NOW YOU CAN READ....

NOAH AND THE ARK

STORY RETOLD BY ELAINE IFE

ILLUSTRATED BY RUSSELL LEE

Published by Rourke Publications, Inc. P.O. Box 868, Windermere, Florida 32786. Copyright © 1983 by Rourke Publications, Inc. All copyrights reserved. No part of this book may be reproduced in any form without written permission from the publisher. Printed in the United States of America.

The Publishers acknowledge permission from Brimax Books for the use of the name "Now You Can Read" and "Large Type For First Readers" which identify Brimax Now You Can Read series.

Library of Congress Cataloging in Publication Data

Ife, Elaine, 1955-
   Noah and the ark.

   (Now you can read—Bible stories)
   Summary: A recounting of the Bible story in which Noah builds a large strong ship to save his family and two of every kind of animal from a flood which covered the earth.
   1. Noah's ark—Juvenile literature.   2. Bible stories, English—O.T. Genesis.   [1. Noah's ark.   2. Bible stories—O.T.   Genesis]   I. Lee, Russell, 1944-   ill.
II. Title.   III. Series.
BS658.I36   1983   222'.1109505   83-13811
ISBN 0-86625-224-X

GROLIER ENTERPRISES CORP.

NOW YOU CAN READ....
NOAH AND THE ARK

Once, long long ago, an old man,
with a long beard and snowy white
hair, was cutting tree trunks into
planks. Many people stood round him
watching to see what he was making.
The man's name was Noah. Noah was
a good man who loved God.

Noah's wife and his three sons watched him work. At last, they saw what he was making. It was a very large, strong ship.

"How can it float?" said Noah's wife. "There is no water nearby." Noah said, "This is a new kind of ship called an ark. It will have a door in the side and a roof. It will have a window and three decks."

"What is it for, husband? Why are you making the ark?" said Noah's wife.

"God has told me to make the ark," said Noah. "He will send rain which will cover the land. Every living thing will die because His people have been wicked. We must go inside the ark with our sons and their children. We must take with us two of every kind of animal. The ark will float on the water and all inside it will be safe."

"We will need food for everyone and food for the animals," said Noah's wife. So, Noah and his wife and three sons began to make plans for their stay in the ark.

Sacks of grain and bags of salt
were put on the deck of the ark.
Barrels of fresh water for drinking
were filled. Hay and straw for the
animals were laid inside the ark.

They found the animals and took
them onto the ark. There was
every kind of animal there,
elephants, lions and camels.

There were dogs, cats, birds,
snakes and even mice and worms.

Noah told everyone to hurry, for
he could see the rain coming. He
pushed two donkeys from behind.
"Come along, you slow donkeys, get
on board if you do not want to
get your feet wet!"

When everyone and everything was inside, Noah closed the door. Soon, great black clouds filled the sky and rain began to fall.

Day after day it rained, until all the land was covered with water. The rain fell for forty days and forty nights. The ark was lifted. It floated high in the water.

The water covered the land for many, many days. Inside the ark, everyone was becoming tired, for it was noisy and there was little food left.

A dog growled, as if to say, "My straw is not soft. I cannot sleep."

On the other side of the ark, the giraffes were very unhappy. The roof was so low that they had to bend their heads. They had very stiff necks.

At last, the rain stopped, and the
waters went down. The ark came to
rest upon a mountain. Noah looked
out to see how he could tell
when it would be safe to leave
the ark.

He went to where the birds rested
and spoke to the big, black raven.
"Go out, raven
and fly over the
land. If you can
find a tree in
which to rest,
then stay there.
If you cannot find
a tree, then fly
back to the ark."
The raven was
away all day. It
did not come
back. "I will wait
a little longer,"
said Noah.

A week later, Noah sent out a dove.

The little dove came back to the ark, for she knew there was food there. "I will wait a little longer," said Noah. "I think things will be better soon."

He waited seven days and let the dove out again.

When night came, Noah saw the dove coming back. It held in its beak a green olive leaf.

"The leaves have grown again on the trees," cried Noah. "Now we can leave the ark."

The door was opened. Noah and his family came out of the ark.

The animals and birds were glad to be free again on dry land. God had spared Noah, and all his family from the flood. They gave thanks to God.

"Look! Look up there in the sky," cried Noah's wife. Right across the sky was a lovely rainbow. This was God's promise that He would never again flood the world.

Sometimes, when it has been raining, if you look up into the sky you, too, can see a rainbow.

All these appear in the pages of the story. Can you find them?

Noah

Noah's wife

ark

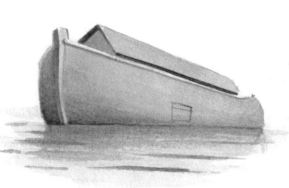

two donkeys

rainbow

dove

mountain

rain

Now tell the story in your own words.